1. Introduction

House price movements are one of the primary drivers of the credit risk associated with mortgage assets. Given this dependence, house price forecasts are an essential component of mortgage risk management in the United States. Over the last half century, real house prices have been characterized by decade long cycles around a positively sloped long-term trend. Because these prices tend to be mean-reverting relative to trend, as house prices rise, the credit risk associated with mortgage assets may increase.[1] To capture this aspect of credit risk it is necessary to consider (1) how far house prices are above long-term trend and (2) the extent to which they can fall below trend. This paper provides a technique for estimating the latter, a conservative lower bound for house prices relative to long-term trend.

The credit risk and required capital associated with mortgage assets is often estimated through stress testing, which entails simulating future loan performance across a series of stressed inputs. These inputs vary across credit models but usually involve, among other variables, a house price path and an interest rate scenario. The house price path is an important determinant of the severity of the stress test, and can be either static or dynamic in nature.

A static path reflects a fixed decline in house price levels, typically based upon prior historical experience (e.g., a 20 percent decline). When applied at different points in the housing cycle, a fixed decline yields different levels of effective stress (the depth of the house price shock relative to long-term trend). As a consequence, a static shock can result in an insufficient level of stress during periods of bubble formation (i.e., where house prices are well above their long-term trend), but an implausible level of stress during market downturns (i.e., where house prices are at or below their long-term trend). For example, the stress scenario employed by the Office of Federal Housing Enterprise Oversight (OFHEO) implemented a fixed house price shock, which proved

---

[1]Mean-reversion has been demonstrated by Capozza et al. (2004), Gao et al. (2009), and Glaeser & Nathanson (2015).

insufficiently stressful in the lead up to the Great Recession. Alternatively, fixed house price shocks based upon the recent crisis but applied in the midst of the recovery (e.g., 2012–present) have resulted in stress scenarios that appear implausible by any historical standard.

In contrast to a fixed house price shock, a dynamic path responds to current market conditions. For instance, a dynamic house price decline is typically governed by where house prices are relative to long-term trend and the extent to which they can fall below this trend (otherwise referred to as the depth of trough). All else equal, a more severe decline, or deeper trough, is associated with a more stressful scenario and higher projected credit losses. An appropriately designed dynamic path can reduce the likelihood of either under- or over-stating the severity of future house price shocks given current market conditions (Smith et al. 2014).

An accurate estimate of the depth of future house price downturns is essential to dynamic stress testing and can be used to evaluate the reasonableness of static stress tests. Our proposed technique to estimate a conservative lower bound (CLB) has two attractive features: it (1) provides a leading indicator of the severity of future crises or the depth of future downturns and (2) allows estimates of trough to recover as markets return to baseline conditions. Both of these features allow for more effective stress testing, which can lead to a more accurate measure of the credit risk associated with all assets backed by single-family mortgages, including new acquisitions, seasoned loans, and all manners of mortgage backed securities.[2]

In estimating a CLB, we begin by examining previous house price cycles and the extent to which prices have fallen below the long-term trend. Figure 1(a) shows three major cycles as real house prices increased over the last thirty years in the United States.[3] Note the relative constancy of the

---

[2]Establishing an accurate measure of credit risk on mortgage assets is potentially useful for several different types of market participants, including institutions with large portfolios of mortgage assets, fiscal planners who advise on real estate investments, individual real estate investors, and financial regulators.

[3]The house price cycles run from 1976 to 1986, 1987 to 2001, and 2002 to present. The underlying house price indexes are a hybrid of the purchase-only and all-transactions indexes constructed by the Federal Housing Finance Agency. A weighted repeat sales methodology is used on approximately 9 million pairings from nearly 25 million

three national troughs (ranging from 7 percent to 10 percent below trend), which is striking given the asymmetry of the associated peaks. Whereas house price peaks are characterized by significant variation across cycles, house price troughs are relatively stable across cycles and can be modeled using a standard set of economic incentives. In brief, as house prices fall below trend, housing becomes an increasingly attractive investment—its well-known mean-reverting nature engenders higher expected returns. Investors and consumers are incented to enter the market, slowly reaching a critical mass of additional demand sufficient to cause house prices to rebound. This phenomenon naturally extends to the state level as illustrated in Figure 1(b), which depicts the distribution of state level troughs across the last three cycles. Distributions are quite similar across cycles with state level troughs typically ranging between five percent and 20 percent below trend.[4]

We have organized our design and tests of a CLB into several sections. Section 2 describes the recent literature related to house price movements. We focus on a specific area: the extent to which house prices can fall. Section 3 introduces a theoretical framework where investors and consumers allocate resources based upon a mean-variance optimization adapted from modern portfolio theory (Markowitz 1952; Freund 1956). Our empirical approach leverages this framework. Section 4 presents regression results and several measures of model fit. Because the CLB has a direct application in dynamic stress testing, we are particularly concerned with not understating the depth of future troughs. This is reflected in our diagnostics, which focus on the under-predictions. Section 5 offers concluding remarks.

---

transactions nationwide of single-family mortgages that have been purchased or securitized by the Fannie Mae or Freddie Mac since 1975. The long-term trend is calculated using a non-linear function of exponential growth. Nominal house prices are converted into real terms using the consumer price index less shelter from the Bureau of Labor Statistics. For the entirety of this paper, we work with a deflated index to remove the noise associated with inflation, which allows us to more precisely identify house price troughs.

[4]The ranges are based upon the 25th and 75th percentiles of the distributions across house price cycles.

Figure 1: Similarities of historical troughs across cycles

(a) National

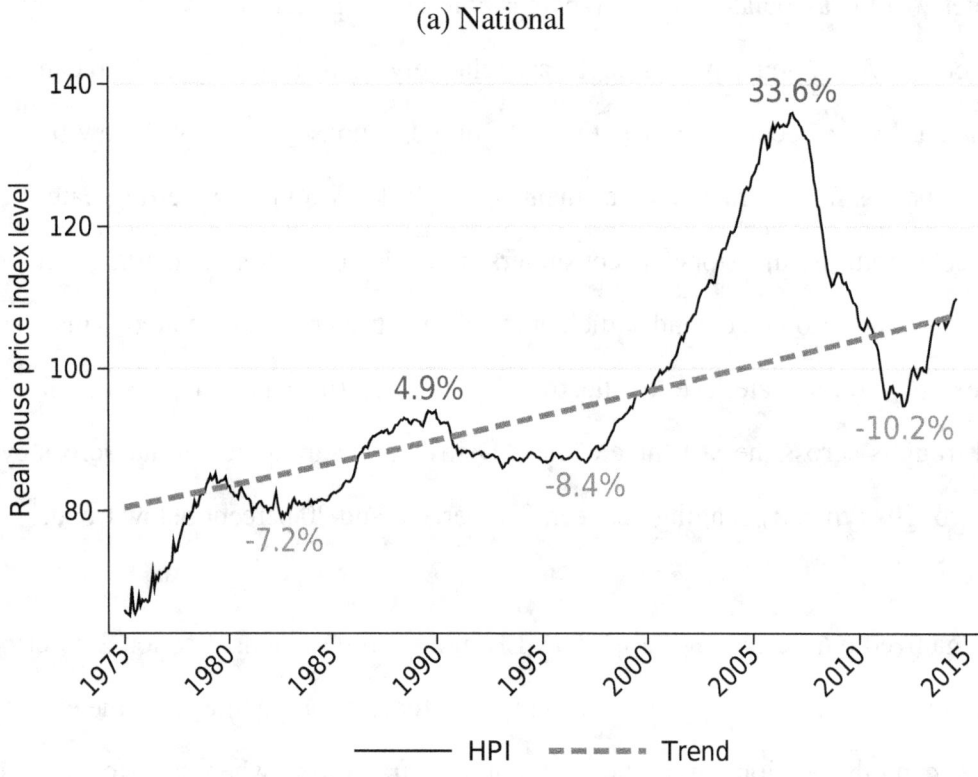

(b) State level

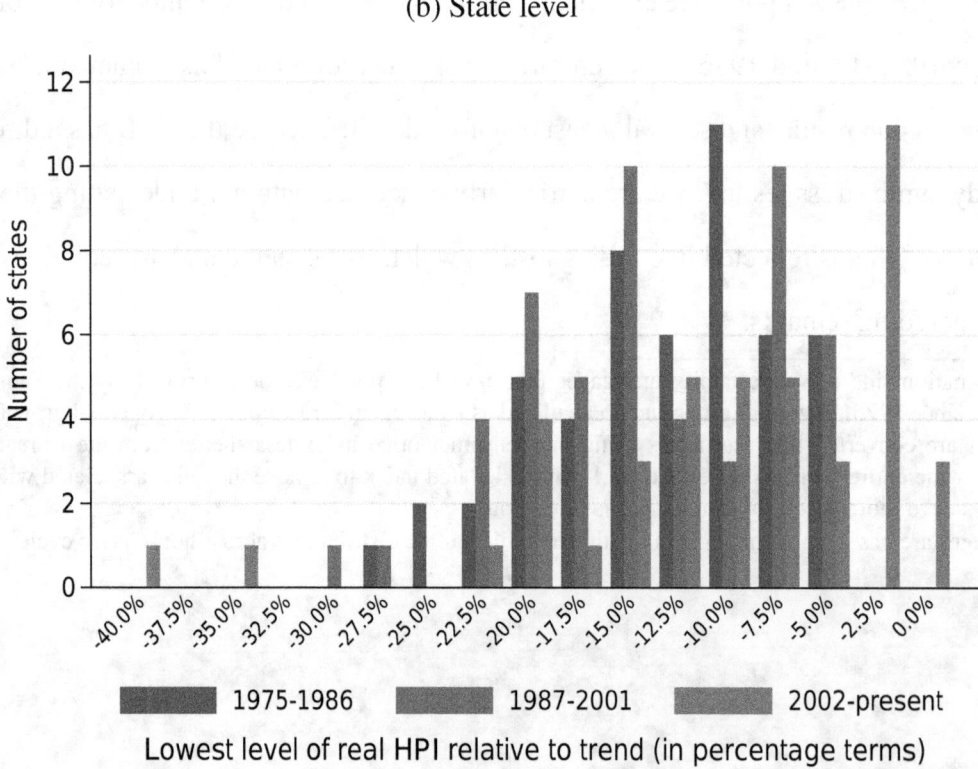

A. Bogin, S. Bruestle, & W. Doerner — How Low Can House Prices Go?

2. Literature Review

The house price literature has developed across several areas since empirical methods for constructing house price indexes were popularized in the 1960s. The recent bubble and subsequent bust have led to a focus on house price dynamics, bubbles, and downturns. Particular attention has been placed on identifying when house prices deviate from a "rational" value based upon market fundamentals and the relationship between several macroeconomic factors and house price changes. Although house prices have begun to stabilize since the Great Recession, the literature offers limited guidance about the dynamics of downturns and the nature and timing of subsequent recoveries. Our paper contributes to this relatively unexplored area and provides new insights into the dynamics and potential depth of housing market downturns.

There is an established body of research on house price dynamics, which includes several topics relevant to our analysis. These include how changing demographics impact housing demand (Mankiw & Weil 1989); the role of construction costs and supply constraints on house price appreciation (Glaeser et al. 2005; Van Nieuwerburgh & Weill 2010; Huang & Tang 2012; Davidoff 2013); and a model that describes house price movements in the context of productivity growth and substitution between housing and non-housing goods (Kahn 2008). The dynamic relationships discussed in these papers between house price levels, the volatility of house prices, and incentives to purchase or invest in housing play an important role in our theoretical foundation that is developed in Section 3. We do this within a utility maximization framework where investors adjust their relative allocations to housing assets because their expected returns and the perceived risk associated with house price volatility change through a cycle.

The recent housing cycle (2001 to present) has prompted research on bubble formation and the role of investor expectations in asset price appreciation. Important studies include the role of excessive expectations of future house price and income growth on bubble formations (Barberis et al. 1998;

Case & Shiller 2003; Shiller 2007; Hoffman et al. 2012) and the impact of Bayesian updating on subjective belief dynamics (Adam et al. 2011). This is a challenging area of study, and there is no current consensus on the dynamics of bubble formation. Nonetheless, researchers agree that investor expectations of future house price appreciation are regularly updated and subject to varying degrees of uncertainty. We attempt to capture these evolving expectations as well as investor uncertainty in our empirical model by incorporating a non-linear investor response function weighted by house price volatility.

Post-crisis, there has been an increasing amount of research on downturns. This includes a survey of the depth and duration of historical financial crises (Reinhart & Rogoff 2009); the introduction of a dynamic stochastic general equilibrium model to forecast future downturn points (Gupta et al. 2011); and several ex-post forecasts of turning points in real housing prices (Rousová & van den Noord 2011; Zietz & Traian 2014). We find, however, that this work does not address the question of how far house prices can fall relative to trend or how we might estimate this lower bound.

As discussed above, several recent papers have developed ex-post techniques for predicting house price downturns. For example, Zietz & Traian (2014) use a Markov switching model to identify when house prices change directions and begin to decrease. Their work is related to our research, but we are focused on pre-emptively estimating the extent to which house prices can fall below trend, and we are less concerned with establishing a precise moment that momentum might change. Rousová & van den Noord (2011) suggest using a probit model to determine when housing prices have reached a trough, but are agnostic as to the severity of the downturn. In the absence of several constraints, their method can lead to misidentifying a local minimum as a global value when a housing cycle is not complete.

While we propose a theoretically supported statistical technique for estimating a CLB, it has also been shown that it is possible to estimate the depth of national and state level troughs solely on

Figure 2: Missing the trough is undesirable

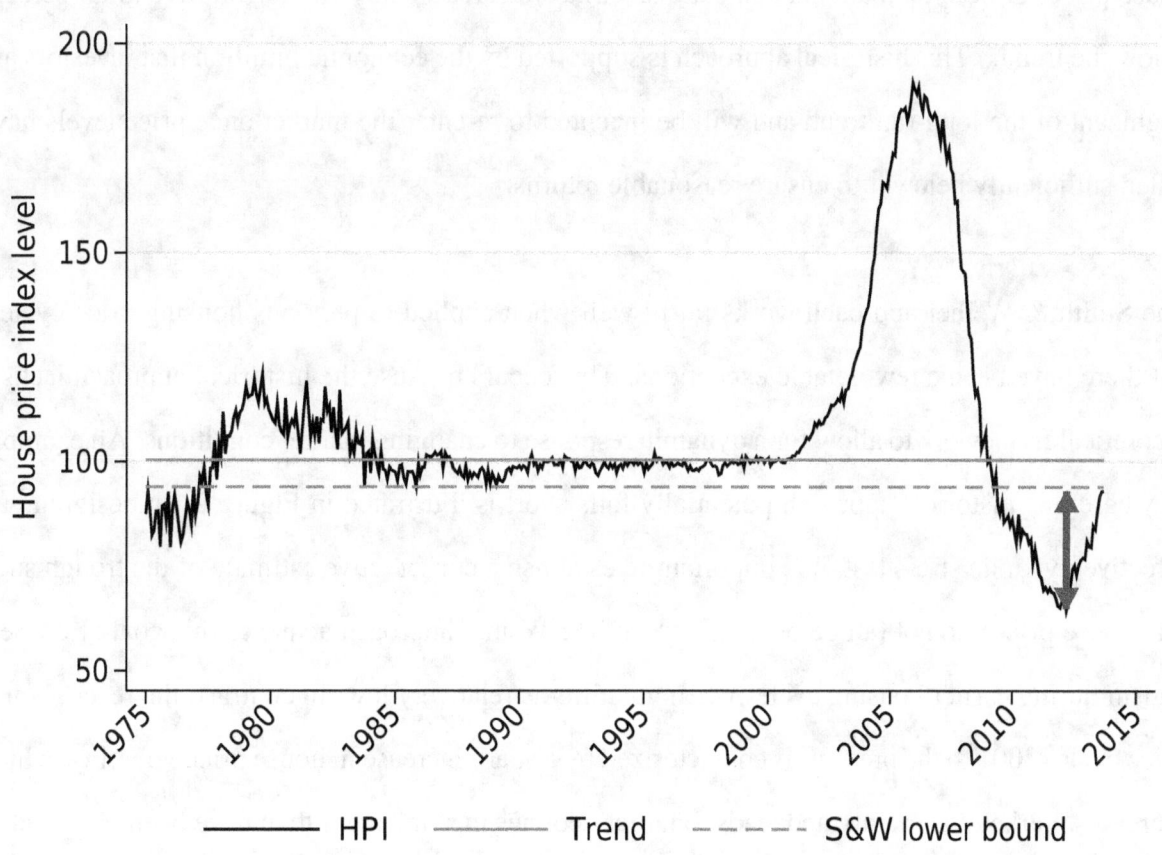

the basis of historical observation. Reinhart & Rogoff (2009) find predictability in the depth of peak-to-trough declines across previous banking crises (on average 35 percent over six years in real terms). Their data, though, represent international house price experiences and do not include the full extent of the recent crisis in the United States. Smith & Weiher (2012) demonstrate with out-of-sample testing that future CLBs can be reasonably estimated at a regional level by assuming a good predictor of trough is the most severe amount that house prices have fallen below trend in previous cycles (as measured in percentage terms). As shown earlier in Figures 1(a) and 1(b), house prices at both the national and state level have decreased anywhere from five to 20 percent below the trend.[5] This historical approach is supported by the economic intuition that investors are cognizant of the long-run trend and will be incented to re-enter the market once price levels have fallen sufficiently below it to ensure reasonable returns.

The Smith & Weiher approach works fairly well when applied to previous housing price cycles, but there have been a few notable exceptions. This occurs because the historical approach lacks a theoretical framework to allow for a dynamic response to changing market conditions. An example of where this historical approach potentially falls short is illustrated in Figure 2. In designing an effective dynamic stress test, it is important to establish a conservative estimate of the trough such that house prices do not fall below it. The Smith & Weiher approach achieves this goal of conservatism during earlier housing cycles when volatility is relatively low. In contrast, the recent house price cycle (2001 to the present) is characterized by a sharp increase in house price volatility, which increases market uncertainty and leads to larger declines in some areas than have been observed in the past. As a result, the Smith & Weiher trough estimates understate actual severities for 10 states (i.e., estimated troughs are shallower than actual troughs). In the context of economic capital, underestimating the severity of state level troughs can lead to an insufficient amount of state-specific risk protection, which represents a major concern for undiversified financial institutions.[6]

---

[5]In contrast, house price peaks have varied considerably across the cycles. At the national level, real house prices rose by only five percent in the late 1980s but by over 30 percent in the last decade.

[6]Another concern might be cases where the trough is overestimated because this represents an inefficient use of capital. Nevertheless, for purposes of risk management, becoming insolvent is much worse than having a lower return

Our model is designed to accommodate changing market conditions, and as such, offers a potential improvement over purely historical approaches such as Smith & Weiher. To our knowledge, this paper is the first attempt at providing a dynamic measure of the depth of future troughs. To highlight the advantages of this approach relative to a static estimate of trough, we compare our CLB results to the Smith & Weiher approach when examining model fit.

3. Theoretical basis and empirical approach

Consider a pool of investors who allocate wealth across three asset classes: housing, bonds and equities, and a risk-free asset such as government debt. Following Freund (1956), each investor solves the following profit maximization problem:

$$E(u_i) = \mu_i - (\alpha_i/2)\sigma_i^2 \tag{1}$$

where μ_i represents the expected return on portfolio i, α_i is an investor specific risk-aversion parameter, and σ_i^2 is the expected variance of returns on portfolio i.[7] Expected return and variance are defined as:

$$\mu_i = W_i \cdot \{E(r_h)x_{hi} + E(r_m)x_{mi} + r_f(1 - x_{hi} - x_{mi})\} \tag{2}$$

$$\sigma_i^2 = W_i^2 \cdot \{E(\sigma_h^2)x_{hi}^2 + E(\sigma_m^2)x_{mi}^2 + 2E(\sigma_{hm})x_{hi}x_{mi}\}. \tag{3}$$

The total share of wealth (W) allocated to each asset class is indicated by x_j where j references housing (h), bonds and equities (m), or a risk free asset (f) such as government debt. $E(r_j)$ and $E(\sigma_j^2)$ indicate the expected returns on each asset class and the volatility or risk associated with holding each in portfolio. To simplify the model, we assume that $\sum W_i = 1$.[8]

---

on capital

[7]Markowitz (1952) embeds a mean-variance approach in modern portfolio theory (MPT). We recognize that our model deviates from the standard MPT that assumes joint elliptical distributions. Instead, we view the investor optimization problem more generally where an asset's variance proxies for risk and the correlations across asset returns provide information regarding the benefits of diversification.

[8]This effectively normalizes total investor wealth.

Investors consider the tradeoff between asset classes and optimize their portfolio by maximizing equations (1), (2), and (3) with respect to h and m. We focus our attention on solving for h, which yields a proxy for housing demand that varies across market environments:

$$argmax(x_h) = \alpha^{-1}[(1 - \rho_{hm})\sigma_h]^{-1}\left[\frac{E(r_h) - r_f}{\sigma_h} - \rho_{hm}\frac{E(r_m) - r_f}{\sigma_m}\right]. \qquad (4)$$

where ρ_{hm} is the expected correlation between h and m.[9] Equation (4) produces several informative comparative statics:

1. A higher degree of risk aversion (α) will mute an investor's response to an increase in the expected return on housing, or $\frac{\partial\, argmax(x_h)}{\partial E(r_h)\partial \alpha_i} < 0$, all else equal.

2. As the expected volatility of housing increases, investors shift away from housing and into other asset classes, or $\frac{\partial\, argmax(x_h)}{\partial E(\sigma_h^2)}) < 0$.

3. If housing and market returns are positively but not perfectly correlated, as the expected return on bonds and equities increases relative to the expected return on housing, investors apportion a greater percentage of their portfolios to these alternate asset classes and decrease their exposure to housing, or $\frac{\partial\, argmax(x_h)}{\partial E(r_m)} < 0$.

Equation (4) and the resulting comparative statics provide a theoretical basis for our empirical approach. Because we are interested in determining a CLB, we embed the investor's maximization problem in our model of housing market downturns as shown below. As house prices fall below long-term trend, housing becomes an increasingly attractive investment relative to other asset classes and investor demand increases.[10] Initially, the least risk-adverse investors (low α) will re-

---

[9]Equation (4) can be simplified by re-expressing several terms as variance-covariance weights, or $argmax(x_h) = \alpha^{-1}\left[\frac{E(r_h)}{w_1} - \frac{E(r_m)}{w_2} - \frac{r_f}{w_3}\right]$ where $w_1 = (1 - \rho_{hm})\sigma_h^2$, $w_2 = \rho_{hm}^{-1}(1 - \rho_{hm})\sigma_h\sigma_m$, and $w_3 = \frac{(1-\rho_{hm})\sigma_h}{\sigma_h^{-1} - \rho_{hm}\sigma_m^{-1}}$.

[10]Assuming house prices are mean-reverting, expected returns can be defined mathematically as a convergence on deviations from trend. Formally, this can be written as $\lim_{T \to \infty}(r_{h,t} - E_t(r_{h,t+T})) = (r_{h,t} - \bar{r}_{h,t+T})$, where $r_{h,t}$ represents real house prices in period t, $E_t(r_{h,t+T})$ is the expectation of real house prices in period $t + T$, and $\bar{r}_{h,t+T}$ is the long-term trend at period $t + T$.

---

enter the market, but as prices continue to fall and the expected return on housing increases, even cautious investors (high α) are incented to re-enter the market.[11] As that occurs, housing demand will ultimately reach a critical mass and engender a recovery. The dynamics of this transition can be expressed as follows:[12,13]

$$y^* = \beta_0 + \beta_1 \left(\frac{1}{\tilde{w}_1}\right) + \sum_{i=1}^{3} \beta_{2,i} \left(\frac{E(HPA_i)}{\tilde{w}_1}\right) + \beta_3 \left(\frac{E(r_m)}{\tilde{w}_2}\right) + \beta_4 \left(\frac{r_f}{\tilde{w}_3}\right) + \gamma \mathbf{M} + \Gamma + \varepsilon \quad (5)$$

where y^* measures how far the current house price index (HPI) level is relative to its actual trough in percentage terms. The tradeoffs between h, m, and f are proxied as follows: the expected returns on housing are measured using the deviation of HPI from long-term trend; the expected returns on equities are approximated using deviations of the price of S&P 500 futures relative to par (r_m); and risk free returns are estimated using the yield on a 10-year constant maturity Treasury bond (r_m).[14,15] Variations across local markets are controlled for with a vector of macroeconomic variables (M). These help us capture differential reactions to house price declines based upon the local market environment (e.g., population growth, real per capita income growth, and unemployment). We control for regional time invariant heterogeneity using census division fixed effects (Γ).

---

[11]A similar idea but a slightly different theoretical approach is developed by Jin & Zhou (2013) where a reference point helps encourage investors with different risk aversion parameters to enter a market.

[12]To make this specification tractable, we use exponentially weighted moving average estimates for the variance-covariance weights that are then transformed as $\tilde{w} = G(t) = \begin{cases} \frac{1}{\omega} + 2(1 - \frac{1}{\omega})t & \text{if } t < \frac{1}{2} \\ \omega + 2(1 - \omega)(1-t) & \text{if } t \geq \frac{1}{2} \end{cases}$ where $t = F\left(\frac{1}{\tilde{w}}\right) \sim U[0,1]$ and ω is chosen to optimize model fit. The weights have three convenient properties: (i) the median of the distribution is normalized to one, (ii) the minimum of the distribution is given a weight of $\frac{1}{\omega}$, and (iii) the maximum of the distribution is given a weight of ω. Property (i) places the coefficients into the median-volatility environment. Property (ii) and (iii) bound any extreme values; therefore, for example, $E(r_h)$ would have no more than ωth the impact and no less than $\frac{1}{\omega}$th the impact than during a median-volatility environment.

[13]The effective impact of this weighting scheme is to narrow the distribution of state-level troughs (relative to trend) on a risk-adjusted basis. Unadjusted, the distribution ranges from -5 to -20 percent, but when we correct for differing levels of volatility within house price cycles the distribution tightens (from -1 to -7 percent).

[14]Fama & French (1989) find that excess returns on corporate bonds and equities move in concert. To extent that this might not occur, we capture investor expectations regarding the future performance of bonds through the risk free rate and a credit spread, which coincides with the business cycle. This spread is proxied for by a combination of the expected returns on equities and the macroeconomic variables.

[15]Because there are only four settle dates for S&P 500 futures contracts during the year, we normalize the expected return on market assets to the expected return over the next year for time t by $E_{1,t}(r_m) = \left[\frac{PS\&P\ Future,t}{PS\&P,t}\right]^{\frac{365}{expiry-t}} - 1$. In the absence of futures data (pre-1982), we proxy for expected returns using the previous year's actual returns.

As illustrated in our first order conditions presented after equation (4), investors are unlikely to respond immediately or simultaneously to changes in expected housing returns. Econometrically, this suggests a non-linear reaction function. Figure 3 shows how we address this concern through two different variables. To measure the distance between current house prices and an observed trough, we construct a dependent variable segmented into six categories (0 to ≤ 5 percent, >5 to ≤ 10 percent, >10 to ≤ 15 percent, >15 to ≤ 20 percent, >20 to ≤ 25 percent and greater than 25 percent such that the percentage denotes the distance from the trough indexed relative to long term trend) as shown in the top panel of Figure 3.[16] This segmentation helps to ensure a sufficient number of state level observations associated with each dependent variable category. Because there is a degree of embedded imprecision when estimating a CLB, we believe that there is little to be gained by producing an exact estimate of trough (e.g., a five percent bandwidth, like 10–15 percent from trough, is more consistent with the certainty of investor expectations than an exact but imprecise estimate, like 12 percent from trough). The bottom panel of Figure 3 illustrates how deviations from trend (our proxy for expected house price appreciation) are translated into a three-part spline function, which allows for a non-linear investor reaction to changes in the expected return on housing.

To estimate our model, we construct a dataset of state level monthly house price movements using a weighted repeat sales methodology that is a hybrid of the purchase-only and all-transactions indexes created by the Federal Housing Finance Agency. Our state level HPI data are created from nearly 25 million raw transactions nationwide of single-family homes that have been sold or refinanced from the mid-1970s thru 2013 (see footnote 3). Given our interest in estimating a CLB, we limit our analysis to downturns with durations of two years or more.[17] This yields a

---

[16]Choosing an alternate number of dependent variable categories (e.g., three or nine) has a negligible impact on estimation results. Goodness of fit statistics are largely unchanged and the number of under-predictions of state-level troughs remains the same.

[17]Alternatively, we could have chosen downturns based on the distance from the long-term trend (instead of the number of years of negative house price appreciation) as done by Borgy et al. (2014). We avoid this specification because it would bind the CLB from above and could severely bias our estimation of the CLB depth depending on the percentage threshold used.

Figure 3: Creating categorical and spline variables

(a) Distance from trough

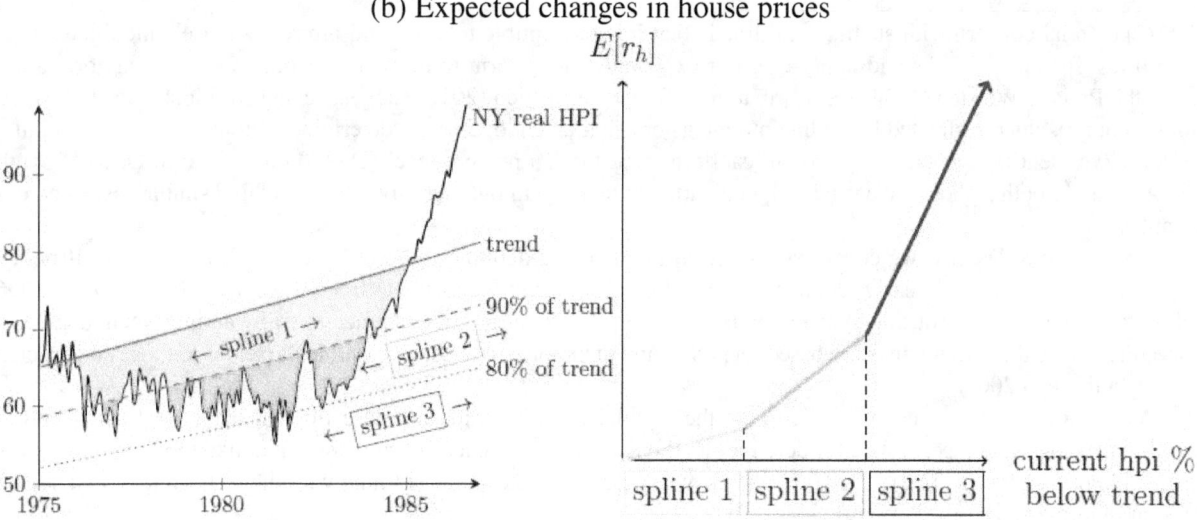

Category ($y =$)	Bounds	Descriptions
I	$y^* \leq \gamma_{\mathrm{I}}$	HPI is 25% or more from trough
II	$\gamma_{\mathrm{I}} < y^* \leq \gamma_{\mathrm{II}}$	HPI is 20-25% from trough
III	$\gamma_{\mathrm{II}} < y^* \leq \gamma_{\mathrm{III}}$	HPI is 15-20% from trough
IV	$\gamma_{\mathrm{III}} < y^* \leq \gamma_{\mathrm{IV}}$	HPI is 10-15% from trough
V	$\gamma_{\mathrm{IV}} < y^* \leq \gamma_{\mathrm{V}}$	HPI is 5-10% from trough
VI	$y^* > \gamma_{\mathrm{V}}$	HPI is 0-5% from trough

(b) Expected changes in house prices

sample size of approximately 8,000 state-month observations, which we split into two datasets to accommodate both in- and out-of-sample testing. The first dataset is truncated at 2001 so we can perform out-of-sample back tests using data from the recent credit crisis.[18] This first sample also makes it possible for a comparison with the Smith & Weiher approach, which uses a trend and trough line constructed with data through 2001.[19] The second dataset extends through late 2013 and allows us to examine the sensitivity of our specification to the choice of sample period.

Our data on state level HPIs are used to construct estimates of the expected return on housing, the expected variance of these returns, and a measure of long term trend. We estimate expected returns on the S&P 500 using data from the Chicago Mercantile Exchange. Our macroeconomic variables are obtained from the U.S. Census Bureau and the Bureau of Labor Statistics.

4. Regression results and model fit

Equation (5) is estimated using an ordered logit technique.[20] The regression results are reported in Table 1. Columns (a) and (b) are based upon data from 49 states and D.C.; columns (c) and (d) exclude five states that show evidence of a structural break in long term trend; and columns (e) and (f) re-introduce these five states with a bifurcated trend line that allows for a structural break

---

[18]A potential concern with such a trend line is that it is susceptible to structural breaks. We use a modified Chow (1960) test for linear breaks and apply it to our exponential long-term trend while accounting for serial correlation using the Prais & Winsten (1954) transformation with one lag. Chien (2010) suggests using additional lags but we do not find our results are affected by adding more lags or using an endogenously determined number of lags. Beginning in 2002, we identify five states with significant breaks at the ten percent level (D.C., Indiana, North Dakota, South Carolina, and South Dakota). We run our specification with and without these five states and find similar results across samples.

[19]Like Smith & Weiher, we construct state-level trends using data through 2001 although alternate cut-off points (e.g., 1999 or 2003) yield nearly identical graphical results. When we estimate trend lines using data through 2006 (close to the peak of the housing cycles), the latter part of the trend lines are characterized by an increasing degree of curvature. Since these trend lines are based on partial and incomplete cycles, we confine ourselves to those constructed with data through 2001.

[20]As part of sensitivity testing, we relaxed the parallel lines assumption and estimated our model using both a multinomial logit and a generalized ordered logit. Predictions were generated and smoothed like those done with the ordered logit (see footnote 23). The CLB results were essentially the same as found with the ordered logit and shown later in Figure 5.

correction.[21] For each set of regressions we estimate over two sample periods, 1976–2001 and 1976–2013, to allow for out-of-sample back-testing. Results are largely consistent across analysis samples, which suggest that our specification captures a fundamental relationship surrounding market downturns that is not simply an artifact of a particular analysis sample or time frame.

The coefficients attached to our control variables are signed as expected and most are statistically significant at the one percent level. Because we are particularly interested in the relationship between the depth of the trough and housing demand, we focus our attention on the coefficient estimates related to expected house price appreciation. The increasing magnitude of the spline coefficients suggests a non-linear response to decreasing housing prices. We interpret this in the context of a heterogeneous group of investors. As house prices fall below trend, an initial cohort of investors re-enters the market because of either low risk aversion or a belief set that house prices will recover quickly. As house prices continue to decline, additional investors re-enter the market as the risk-return profile of housing assets becomes more universally attractive. Eventually a critical mass develops and house prices begin to increase back towards trend. Such behavior is consistent with the widely held belief that house prices are mean-reverting.

---

[21]Michigan has been excluded from this analysis because of an abnormally long 13-year downturn, which led to complications involving our estimating equation's third spline term and made it difficult to estimate post-period trend.

Table 1: Ordered logit regression results

| Variables | All states | | | | No states with structural breaks | | | | Adjusting for structural breaks | | | |
| | (a) 1976-2001 | | (b) 1976-2013 | | (c) 1976-2001 | | (d) 1976-2013 | | (e) 1976-2001 | | (f) 1976-2013 | |
	Coefficient	SE	Coefficient	SE	Coefficient	SE	Coefficient	SE	Coefficient	SE	Coefficient	SE
HPI variance (β_1)	1.582***	0.106	1.894***	0.114	1.303***	0.106	1.831***	0.117	1.582***	0.127	1.934***	0.117
HPI spline 1 ($\beta_{2,1}$)	35.081***	0.750	26.384***	0.805	36.251***	0.762	28.601***	0.953	35.081***	1.007	27.013***	0.953
HPI spline 2 ($\beta_{2,2}$)	79.954***	1.491	54.492***	1.563	77.628***	1.522	54.056***	2.066	79.954***	2.153	56.124***	2.066
HPI spline 3 ($\beta_{2,3}$)	127.626***	7.725	61.690***	7.505	121.895***	7.752	54.957***	13.026	127.626***	13.061	61.199***	13.026
S&P 500 (β_3)	-1.583	0.870	-1.641*	0.918	-2.885***	0.872	-2.872***	1.035	-1.583	1.084	-1.512*	1.035
S&P 500 proxy ($\beta_{3pr\text{-}83}$)	0.472	0.702	-0.105	0.730	0.159	0.703	-0.502	0.820	0.472	0.834	-0.154	0.820
risk-free rate (β_4)	2.952**	1.150	-0.37	1.246	3.548**	1.162	1.038	1.473	2.952**	1.567	-0.383	1.473
population, 1-year	11.242***	0.999	12.475***	1.045	11.274***	1.000	10.235***	1.146	11.242***	1.199	11.958***	1.146
population, 10-year	-10.334***	1.009	-11.782***	1.053	-10.416***	1.010	-9.655***	1.156	-10.334***	1.206	-11.272***	1.156
income, 1-year	4.784***	0.916	3.770***	1.005	5.095***	0.918	5.370***	1.013	4.784***	1.124	4.121***	1.013
income, 10-year	-5.610***	0.920	-3.299***	1.002	-5.354***	0.922	-4.08***	1.018	-5.610***	1.116	-3.637***	1.018
unemployment, 1-year	-0.014	0.020	0.035*	0.022	0.014	0.020	0.073***	0.025	-0.014	0.027	0.037*	0.025
unemployment, 10-year	-0.273***	0.027	-0.147***	0.029	-0.273***	0.027	-0.176***	0.031	-0.273***	0.033	-0.151***	0.031
New England	0.996***	0.111	1.232***	0.114	0.982***	0.111	1.082***	0.128	0.996***	0.131	1.213***	0.128
Middle Atlantic	1.068***	0.132	1.458***	0.132	1.062***	0.132	1.459***	0.151	1.068***	0.152	1.456***	0.151
East North Central	1.574***	0.131	1.304***	0.138	1.160***	0.132	0.976***	0.156	1.574***	0.162	1.255***	0.156
West North Central	0.896***	0.139	1.390***	0.144	1.202***	0.139	1.528***	0.160	0.896***	0.165	1.342***	0.160
South Atlantic	1.556***	0.108	1.596***	0.110	1.573***	0.108	1.506***	0.126	1.556***	0.128	1.551***	0.126
East South Central	1.438***	0.138	1.688***	0.142	1.737***	0.139	1.849***	0.161	1.438***	0.165	1.624***	0.161
West South Central	-0.56***	0.122	-0.044	0.125	-0.384***	0.122	0.097	0.139	-0.560***	0.142	-0.072	0.139
Mountain	0.267**	0.114	0.265**	0.117	0.401***	0.114	0.370***	0.125	0.267**	0.128	0.246**	0.125
γ_I	-2.966	1.712	9.791	1.954	2.374	1.714	17.186	2.035	-2.966	2.428	9.863	2.035
γ_{II}	-1.249	1.708	11.454	1.950	4.075	1.709	18.829	2.029	-1.249	2.422	11.527	2.029
γ_{III}	0.404	1.707	13.13	1.950	5.665	1.709	20.466	2.026	0.404	2.419	13.206	2.026
γ_{IV}	2.586	1.710	14.975	1.953	7.754	1.711	22.259	2.026	2.586	2.419	15.061	2.026
γ_V	5.337	1.713	17.365	1.958	10.501	1.714	24.696	2.027	5.337	2.421	17.466	2.027
Observations	8,232		7,486		8,232		7,486		7,272		8,232	
Number of states	50		50		45		45		50		50	
Pseudo R^2	0.263		0.267		0.266		0.267		0.319		0.266	

Note: For columns (a) and (b), the "all states" regressions include the District of Columbia and every state in the United States except for Michigan. Michigan has been excluded because of complications with the third HPI spline term (it had a thirteen year downturn from the early 1980s to 1990s). Columns (c) and (d) remove five states (D.C., Indiana, North Dakota, South Dakota, and South Carolina) because they show evidence of a structural break at a .10 significance level. Columns (e) and (f) correct for the structural breaks and re-estimations are performed on the full sample (except for Michigan). The levels of significance are defined as * for $p = .10$, ** for $p = .05$, and *** for $p = .001$.

After estimating equation (5), we calculate dynamic state level CLBs through a counterfactual exercise: (1) for each month of our state level time series, we hold our control variables constant while simultaneously decreasing real house prices until our model predicts we are within five percent of trough. This is an iterative procedure where house prices are incrementally decreased until the estimated probability of being in category six (0-5 percentage points from trough) is greater than or equal to 95 percent; (2) because of the bandwidth associated with our categorical dependent variable, we then lower real house prices an additional five percentage points.[22,23] This exercise provides us with a CLB for state level house prices that varies across the housing cycle and market environments.

In Table 2, we examine several measures of model fit to explore the efficacy of our specification across a number of metrics. Panel (a) presents modified concordance statistics that measure the extent to which estimated troughs align with actual troughs. We perform this exercise both in- and out-of-sample. Panel (b) details the frequency of under-predictions of actual trough severity over the last two housing cycles.

Modified concordance (C) statistics allow us to assess our model's discriminative ability. The first three rows of Table 2(a) illustrate how often our model successfully identifies actual troughs (true positive tests). Specifically, given that house prices are within five percentage points of actual trough, we identify how often our model estimates house prices are within five, 10, and 15 percentage points of trough. The associated concordance statistics suggest a high degree of fit, or that the model successfully identifies that house prices are within ten percentage points of the trough more than 95 percent of the time in-sample and 71 percent of the time out-of-sample.[24] The last row of Table 2(a) illustrates how often our model correctly predicts that house prices are not at

---

[22]The coarseness of this bandwidth permits house prices to drop up to an additional five percentage points after reaching category six. We hedge against this uncertainty by decreasing house prices an additional five percentage points.

[23]After computing an initial set of CLB estimates, we smooth each state-level time series using kernel-weighted local polynomial smoothing.

[24]The out-of-sample dataset runs from 2002 to 2013 and provides a measure of our model's future predictive ability.

Table 2: Measures of model fit

(a) Concordance statistics

Concordance statistics	Range	In-Sample: 1976–2013	Out-of-sample: 2002–2013
True-Positives	0–5 percentage points from trough	69.70%	45.70%
	0–10 percentage points from trough	95.90%	71.30%
	0–15 percentage points from trough	99.50%	99.70%
True-Negatives	More than 5 percentage points from trough	84.60%	82.50%

Note: The percentages represent the CLB is within a certain range of actual HPI given that the actual HPI is within 5 percentage points of actual trough (for true-positives) or more than 5 percentage points of actual trough (for true-negatives). Coefficients are estimated with data through 2013 for the in-sample tests and through 2001 for the out-of-sample tests.

(b) Number of under-predicted troughs

	S&W (2012)	CLB
Last Full House Price Cycle (1987–2001)	32	0
Great Recession (2008–2013)	10	3

Note: The CLB results here are the same when estimated with all states or dropping those with structural breaks (i.e., columns (a) and (c) for the first row above on the last full house price cycle and (b) and (d) for the second row above on the Great Recession). The CLBs associated with the second row above on the Great Recession are estimated out-of-sample. Re-estimations using adjustments for structural breaks still return 0 under-predictions for the last full house price cycle and 4 under-predictions for the Great Recession but those data are in-sample tests (i.e., data through 2013).

trough (true-negative tests). As shown, when actual house prices are more than five percentage points from trough, our model correctly predicts house prices are not at trough 84 percent of the time in-sample and 82 percent of the time out-of-sample.

With the understanding that our estimates of the CLB have been designed in support of stress testing, we are more concerned with under-predicting than over-predicting actual troughs. Over-predicting the depth of the trough can lead to an inefficient use of capital while under-predicting the depth of trough can potentially lead to insolvency. As a result of this asymmetry, we want to err on the side of conservatism, which means focusing on the extent of under-prediction.

Table 2(b) illustrates how often our CLB estimates underestimate actual trough over the last two housing cycles. As a point of comparison, we include a similar measure based on the Smith & Weiher approach as discussed in Section 2. During the last full house price cycle (1987–2001), the simpler Smith & Weiher approach (for this comparison, based upon actual data through 1986) under-predicts 31 of the 49 states and D.C. In contrast, the CLB understates zero states. Figures 4(a) and 4(b) provide more detail with a state-by-state comparison of predicted versus actual troughs. Deviations above the horizontal axis (centered at zero percent) represent under-predictions of trough, while deviations below the horizontal axis represent overly conservative predictions (i.e., the actual trough is above its estimated value).

Figure 4(a) reiterates the conservative nature of the CLB with all trough estimates (blue bars) lying slightly below the horizontal axis. In contrast, over half of Smith & Weiher's trough estimates (red bars) are above the horizontal axis indicating a considerable number of under-estimates. This could lead financial institutions that lack geographic diversification (e.g., that have a majority of mortgage assets with origins in California or Texas) to undercapitalize. Note, the negative impact of under-estimating state level troughs could potentially be muted for well-diversified institutions through cross-subsidization (e.g., capital requirements may be understated for holdings in California

Figure 4: Lowest level of real house prices relative to trough

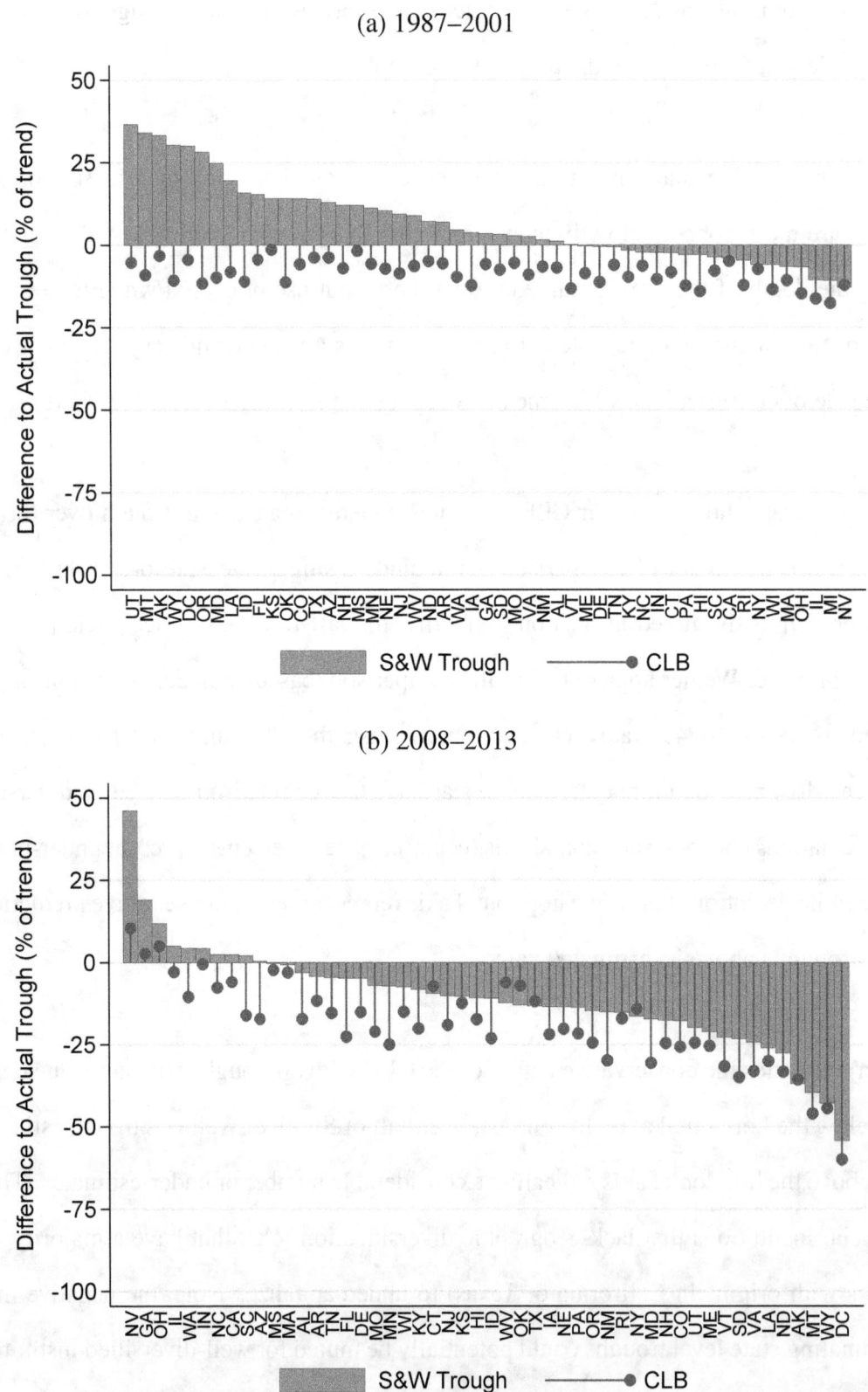

(a) 1987–2001

(b) 2008–2013

A. Bogin, S. Bruestle, & W. Doerner — How Low Can House Prices Go?

or Texas but overstated for holdings in New York and Pennsylvania).

Table 2(b) also presents the extent of under-predictions during the recent housing crisis (from 2008 onward). Relative to the previous cycle, the Smith & Weiher predictions improve but still understate observed troughs in 10 states.[25] As designed, the CLB provides a cautious view of the potential severity of state level downturns by only under-estimating three states. The CLB's performance is even more noteworthy given that the post-2001 estimates are performed out-of-sample. With enough parameters, variables, and a properly specified model, in-sample estimates should closely align with actual observations because they are calibrated to the entire dataset. This, though, is not necessarily indicative of future model performance. Out-of-sample testing allows us to gauge how well our model would perform in the future without such foreknowledge. In other words, even with data only through 2001 and not knowing how the ensuing Great Recession would unfold, our CLB approach is still able to successfully identify the extent of housing market downturns in almost all states.

The success of the CLB approach is partially a function of its ability to adapt to changing market conditions. For example, during the last housing cycle, a significant increase in Nevada's house price volatility led to an increase in the estimated severity of the state's CLB. As illustrated in Figure 4(b), our approach is able to successfully forecast the actual and precipitous decline in house prices, even though they significantly exceeded the previous historical precedent. Out-of-sample, the CLB method only understates the severity of Nevada's house price decline by 6.6 percent. In comparison the Smith & Weiher approach under-estimates Nevada's actual house price decline by over 30 percentage points. This shows the dynamic adjustment feature of the CLB approach works extremely well in capturing steep declines even when it is calibrated with data reflecting the more modest nature of previous house price cycles.

---

[25]The improvement results from updating the Smith & Weiher methodology to incorporate the observed severity of state-level troughs through 2001. This model error correction results in fewer states being underestimated for the Great Recession (2008–2013).

Figure 5: Comparing the CLB with Smith and Weiher (2012)

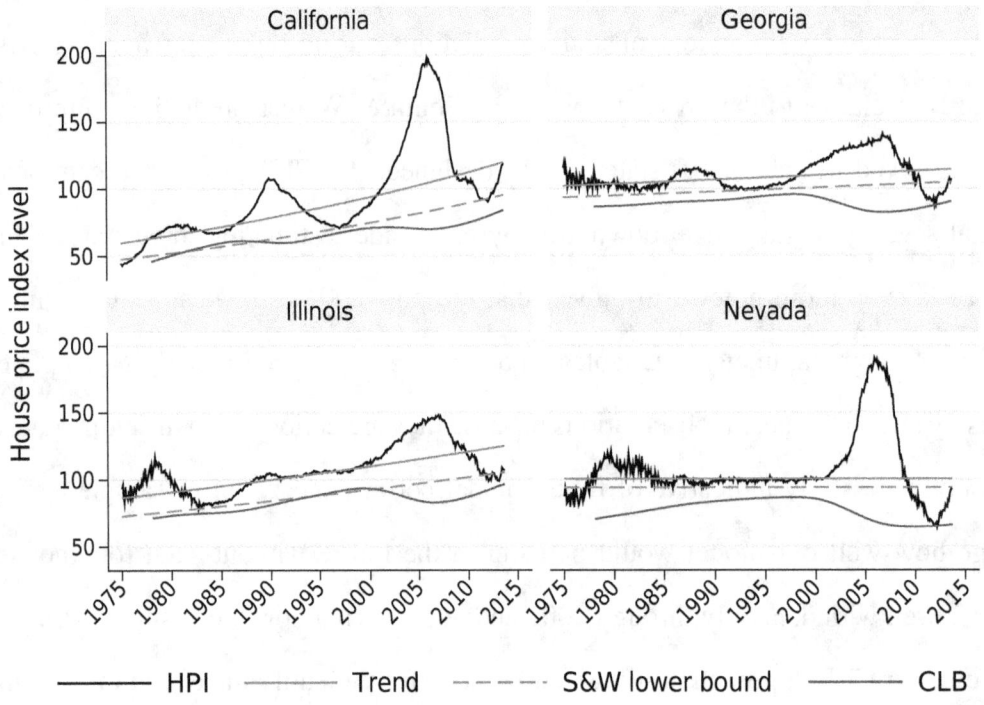

Figure 6: A potential early warning indicator of future housing downturns

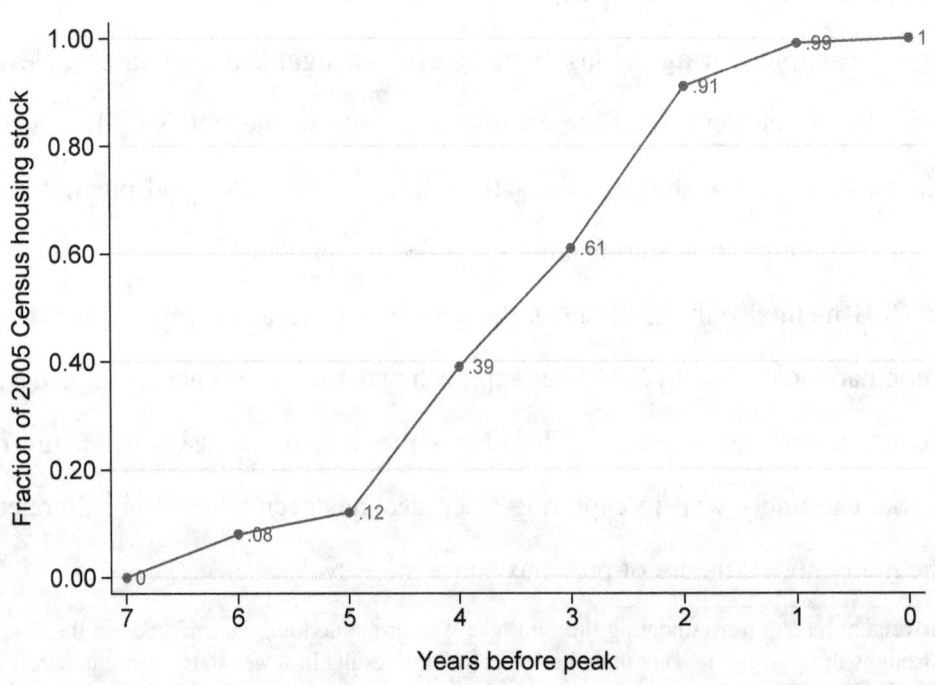

Figure 5 demonstrates how our state-level CLBs evolve over time. Four sets of CLB estimates are shown to illustrate in-sample performance across several market environments (California, Georgia, Illinois, and Nevada). For three of these four states, the CLB is successful at closely approximating state specific downturns. The CLB slightly overstates the severity of the recent downturns in California and Illinois, but successfully captures the large decline in Georgia and Nevada. As discussed above, the change in Nevada's estimated trough is partially driven by the increase in house price volatility over the last cycle.

Because the CLB begins to fall before house prices reach their peak, it could also act as an early warning sign of a future housing downturn. Graphically, the CLB appears to indicate a subsequent downturn when, after moving away from the long-term trend, its rate of decline begins to slow down. To illustrate how this could be applied to the most recent cycle, we followed several criteria: post-2000, the CLB has moved away from the trend (for at least three quarters and it is at least 15 percent below trend) and the rate of decline begins to slow down (or it inflects). To further isolate prospective bubbles, we also require that the HPI is at least 5 percentage points above trend. When these criteria are applied, the CLB early warning indicator is able to identify potential problems well before house prices peak. As shown in Figure 6, downturns can be detected at least two years prior to a peak for 90 percent of the housing stock (based upon 2005 Census estimates).[26]

Such a leading indicator could encourage financial institutions to build up sufficient capital reserves in advance of a downturn, and the CLB is slightly more conservative than would happen under Smith & Weiher. In summary, the CLB offers an empirically driven but cautious view of market downturns, which can be useful in various stress testing applications.

---

[26]Using these criteria, the CLB can indicate future downturns in the majority of states during the most recent crisis. Exceptions occur when house prices are flat (e.g. Texas and Oklahoma) or when the CLB does not inflect (Hawaii). To increase conservativism, these criteria could be supplemented by additional indicators, like when house prices rise a certain percentage above trend.

5. Concluding remarks and discussion

Since the recent financial crisis, there has been an increasing focus on improving stress testing. Thus far, the stressed housing paths have been largely static in nature, essentially ignoring current market conditions. This paper proposes a conservative lower bound with a theoretical foundation that is supported by empirical evidence. Our CLB approach provides a dynamic path that would vary with market conditions. The regression results compare the efficacy of this approach relative to the historical precedent approach of Smith & Weiher across two different housing cycles where the underlying data cover house price transactions across the United States. As demonstrated, the CLB is able to adapt successfully to changing market conditions and acts as a leading indicator for future market downturns. In addition to accurately capturing the severity of downturns, it also allows estimated troughs to recover as markets return to baseline conditions. The approach performs well in both in-sample and out-of-sample historical back-testing. Although it is more complicated to implement than the Smith & Weiher method, the CLB reduces the potential for understating the extent of future state-level house price declines, allowing for more accurate stress testing.

While we concentrate on modeling house price movements, our CLB approach could also be applied to other asset classes characterized by cyclical movements and mean-reverting properties. Future research might further explore structural breaks in long-term trends or modeling house price downturns at a more granular level (e.g., MSA, county, zip code). This area of work is particularly important for evaluating the reasonableness of static stress tests or developing dynamic stress tests that could help prepare financial institutions for low probability but high impact events such as the recent financial crisis.

References

Adam, K., Kuang, P., & Marcet, A. (2011). House price booms and the current account. Tech. rep., NBER. Working Paper 17224.

Barberis, N., Shleifer, A., & Vishny, R. (1998). A model of investor sentiment. *Journal of Financial Economics*, *49*, 307–343.

Borgy, V., Clerc, L., & Renne, J.-P. (2014). Measuring aggregate risk: Can we robustly identify asset-price boom-bust cycles? *Journal of Banking & Finance*, *46*, 132–150.

Capozza, D. R., Hendershott, P. H., & Mack, C. (2004). An anatomy of price dynamics in illiquid markets: Analysis and evidence from local housing markets. *Real Estate Economics*, *32*, 1–32.

Case, K. E. & Shiller, R. J. (2003). Is there a bubble in the housing market? *Brooking Papers on Economic Activity*, 299–362.

Chien, M.-S. (2010). Structural breaks and the convergence of regional house prices. *Journal of Real Estate Finance and Economics*, *40*, 77–88.

Chow, G. C. (1960). Tests of equality between sets of coefficients in two linear regressions. *Econometrica*, *28*, 591–605.

Davidoff, T. (2013). Supply elasticity and the housing cycle of the 2000s. *Real Estate Economics*, *41*, 793–813.

Fama, E. F. & French, K. R. (1989). Business conditions and expected returns on stocks and bonds. *Journal of Financial Economics*, *25*, 23–49.

Freund, R. J. (1956). The introduction of risk into a programming model. *Econometrica*, *24*, 253–263.

Gao, A., Lin, Z., & Na, C. F. (2009). Housing market dynamics: Evidence of mean reversion and downward rigidity. *Journal of Housing Economics*, *18*, 256–266.

Glaeser, E. L., Gyourko, J., & Saks, R. E. (2005). Why have housing prices gone up? *The American Economic Review*, *95*, 329–333.

Glaeser, E. L. & Nathanson, C. G. (2015). An extrapolative model of house price dynamics. Tech. rep., NBER. Working Paper 21037.

Gupta, R., Kabundi, A., & Miller, S. M. (2011). Forecasting the US real house price index: Structural and non-structural models with and without fundamentals. *Economic Modelling*, *28*, 2013–2021.

Hoffman, M., Krause, M. U., & Laubach, T. (2012). Trend growth expectations and U.S. house prices before and after the crisis. *Journal of Economic Behavior & Organization*, *83*, 394–409.

Huang, H. & Tang, Y. (2012). Residential land use regulation and the US housing price cycle between 2000 and 2009. *Journal of Urban Economics*, *71*, 93–99.

Jin, H. & Zhou, X. Y. (2013). Greed, leverage, and potential losses: A prospect theory perspective. *Mathematical Finance*, *23*, 122–142.

Kahn, J. A. (2008). What drives house prices? Tech. rep., Federal Reserve Bank of New York Staff Reports. No. 345.

Mankiw, G. N. & Weil, D. N. (1989). The baby boom, the baby bust, and the housing market. *Regional Science and Urban Economics*, *19*, 235–258.

Markowitz, H. M. (1952). Portfolio selection. *Journal of Finance*, *7*, 77–91.

Prais, S. & Winsten, C. (1954). Trend estimators and serial correlation. Tech. rep., Cowles Foundation. Discussion Paper 383.

Reinhart, C. M. & Rogoff, K. S. (2009). The aftermath of financial crises. Tech. rep., NBER. Working Paper 14656.

Rousová, L. & van den Noord, P. (2011). Predicting peaks and troughs in real house prices. Tech. rep., OECD Economics Department Working Papers. No. 882.

Shiller, R. J. (2007). Understanding recent trends in house prices and homeownership. *Proceedings - Economic Policy Symposium - Jackson Hole, Federal Reserve Bank of Kansas City*, 89–123.

Smith, S., Fuller, D., Bogin, A., Polkovnichenko, N., & Weiher, J. (2014). Countercyclical capital regime revisited: Tests of robustness. Tech. rep., Federal Housing Finance Agency, Washington, DC. Working Paper 14-1.

Smith, S. & Weiher, J. (2012). Countercyclical capital regime: A proposed design and empirical evaluation. Tech. rep., Federal Housing Finance Agency, Washington, DC. Working Paper 12-2.

Van Nieuwerburgh, S. & Weill, P.-O. (2010). Why has house price dispersion gone up? *The Review of Economic Studies*, *77*, 1567–1606.

Zietz, J. & Traian, A. (2014). When was the U.S. housing downturn predictable? A comparison of univariate forecasting methods. *The Quarterly Review of Economics and Finance*, *54*, 271–281.